FEELINGS

FEELINGS

Jean Goldstein, Tao Yin

VANTAGE PRESS
New York

Cover design by Aaron Fuchs

FIRST EDITION

Published by Vantage Press, Inc.
419 Park Ave. South, New York, NY 10016

Manufactured in the United States of America
ISBN: 0-533-14960-6

Library of Congress Catalog Card No.: 2004093758

0 9 8 7 6 5 4 3 2 1

This work, which is not only an in-depth investigation of the human experience, but also a realistic assessment of the thoughts, the feelings, the hopes, the dreams, and the fantasies of one who is beyond the point of no return, is dedicated to my beloved husband, Harold, and my wonderful daughter, Robyn, whose love and support have given me the vision, the courage, and the strength to complete the anthology, *Feelings.*

Contents

Prose Poetry II

Author's Reflections

To create poetry that has substance, depth, and spirituality is one challenge, but to probe within yourself to find the answers to the following questions is perhaps even more difficult. For . . .

What are feelings? What is their role? From what do they emanate? And are they not only the very essence of our beings, but also the outer extensions of our conscious and subconscious. To be more explicit, the human condition, as it endeavors to deal with the difficult complexities found in every moment, every hour of our daily lives, of our very existence.

Happiness-sadness, love-hate, beauty-ugliness, positive-negative, religious-atheistic, fidelity-infidelity, selfishness-unselfishness, all these feelings and many many more, ad infinitum—all diametrically opposed to each other (Japanese philosophy of aesthetics), they are intrinsically revealed in the individual's total demeanor, mentally, emotionally, spiritually, and physically.

Not only that, but it appears that there are varying levels of feelings, and that they change constantly as one acquires depth and understanding, the basic truths of what it means to be human, in the truest sense of the word.

For it appears feelings reflect who you really are, what you are made of, your deepest reactions as a result of your everyday experiences, your ups and downs, and your negatives and your positives. Also, they are the reflections of whether or not you are living life to its fullest or just existing. Whether or not you have achieved the ability to change, to have elasticity, and to be flexible regardless of your problems and difficulties. And, lastly, but most importantly, whether or not you choose to exist with hate, cynicism, negativism, selfishness, greed, loneliness, or the desire to live life with love, hope, positiveness, courage, wisdom, compassion, understanding, humility, and happiness. Indeed, all the vital expressions of the human psyche, the human experience. In other words, your "Feelings."

FEELINGS

Poetry I

The Cycle

Like the branches of the giant fir
I reach out my arms to the sun
I touch the living buds that will bloom
I know the cycle has begun.

Like on the wings of the blackest, whitest crane
the days of my years fly by
and like the autumn leaves that shine so bright
then wither away and die.

Like the flower that's born to bloom in the spring
its star rises but once a year
then is crushed into dust as nature's life force
renews itself and the miracle reappears.

But I, unlike the flower, in my deepest knowledge
I know that my star will be
only once, perhaps once, in my lifetime
for all the world to feel and hear and see.

And then like the roar of thunder on a summer's night
I will give my last hurrah
or like the brightest of a cricket's light
I will be the rainbow from afar.

Or perhaps, if I could, I would choose to be
that giant fir from my family's tree
or perhaps, if I could, I would choose to be
the beauty and form of a bonsai tree.

And perhaps, if I could, I would choose to be
the quiet at the end of the storm
or the sweetest song of the whippoorwill
in the early September morn.

But alas, I mere man am the fool of life
one chance, perhaps, one chance do I have to be
great or small, short or tall
I cannot change my destiny.

For my lot is cast, my song will be sung
my karma for all to see
for I am mere man, I cannot change
what was, what is, and what will be!

With

With my eyes I touch all nature's forms
For my eyes are meant to see
With my lips I say the kindest words
For my lips are meant to be
With my ears I hear all nature's call
For my ears were meant to hear
When my heart sings the chant of love to you
Then we're one, and I have no fear.

With my soul I try to touch the sun
As it warms the earth it will
Warm your heart, my love,
And give life to everyone.

But will our souls live on and on I ask
Like the stars and the moon that
Glow in the sky
Or will our thoughts, our spirit our hearts
Live on only to wither away and die.

There is no answer, I do not know, my love
Yet somehow it seems we were meant to be
More than the past and the present, a part of eternity.

The Butterfly

Like the butterfly, I dance in the wind
On the wings of song, I soar above the clouds
And when the air is warm and silent
I flit from flower to flower as I
Ponder my fate
Who is the master of my soul, I ask
The butterfly, am I?

In Reverence and Humility

In reverence and humility, I lift up
my eyes to see
the beauty of all nature and the beauty
that is yet to be.

The darks, the lights, the shadows on the wall
the whites and browns and blacks and blues
the great, the in between, the small
the real, the true or false, the rights
or wrongs, let me also see
or I will be lost in my world, my human world
no chance to fulfill my sacred
destiny.

In reverence and humility, I open
my lips to speak
of the goodness and kindness of all mankind
of the strong and of the weak
with my lips let me share, let me
spread the call, let me try to say
what is right
let me cast away my doubts and despair
and let love and hope replenish the days
and the nights.

In reverence and humility, let me listen to
nature's joyous song
to the whispered word of earth's living things
to the power and majesty of the lion's roar
to the owl's hoot, to the cricket's chirp
the croaking of the lonesome frog
I hear the voices of all the world
the rippling brook, the ocean's beat
even the quiet sound of the fog.

And then I hear the melody of the pure
undaunted snow,
the pelting rain, the roll of thunder and
the rumblings of the earth below,
the waterfalls, the cuckoo's call, the song
of the robin as it sings of hope,
of life's renewal in the world
of earthly things.

And then when all is quiet and nature's
task is through, I hear the desperate call
of man to change what's old to new,
to let me hear what I have to hear,
to let me really see what I have to see,
to let my lips finally speak the truth
with courage and faith and honesty.

Then when all this is said and done
let my hands create a miracle,
give my hands the wisdom of life,
let me mold the old
into the new and obliterate
violence and hatred and strife.

And then at long last let my heart beat the
drum of the drummer boy
let my soul sing the song of love
on the wings of the mighty eagle
let my voice soar high above
let it touch the clouds, let it touch
the stars, let the song sing on and on
let the bells ring, let the voice sing
its song, sing its song, on and on.

I Wonder

I wonder how I wonder
Why my thoughts reach out to you
Why each hour of each day has
A special meaning
Whether we don't or whether we do.

I wonder how I wonder
Why my life's pendulum swings to the left and
Then to the right
Why my waking moments go up and down
From dawn 'til dusk.
'Til your love covers me in the darkness
Of the night.

I wonder how I wonder
Without you what my life would be
An empty song, a nothing cry, an empty
Symphony.

And I wonder how I wonder
How you came to guide my way
How you came to unlock my mind,
My heart, my soul
And give meaning and substance to each
Passing day
And then when my daily chores are through
When my tasks are complete, and I have no more
I wonder will I still have you, my love
Or will my life be the same, a lonely
And useless life, the same as it was before.

I Look at the World

I look at the world with my naked eyes
I think of what will be
I cry with my eyes, those naked eyes
For all I see is distrust and inhumanity
Dishonesty dismay almost hopelessness
Confused, I ask what can I do
To change this ugly, distorted world of man
To change from the old to the new.

I look at the world with my naked dreams
I turn away once again in despair
For I cannot look at what I dream of
A world beyond repair.

I listen to the world with my naked ears
I hear sounds that I don't want to hear
Cries of violence, cries of mental and physical pain
And the sudden blast of the gun in my ear
And then the sounds of the sirens, all kinds of
Sirens
Carrying a message to those who walk
Happy and free
That they must assume the role,
Take the challenge
They must try to change what I hear, what I
Think and what I see.

For they must take the world, turn it upside down
Turn it inside out to the left and to the right
Shake up the rich as well as the poor
And give them time to find the light
Then let the wheels of urgent change
Begin their task again and be joined
By the partnership of things and nature
And men.
Then once again when I look with
My naked eyes
When I dream and hear without guilt
Without shame
I will know in my heart and soul
The efforts of my life and yours would not
Have been in vain.

My Mirror

My mirror speaks to me
of what is real and what is true
it talks to me of many things
and tries to tell me what to say and
what to do.

It speaks of facial lines that twist and turn
of eyes scarred with circles and with rings
of age, of drastic changes,
of wrinkles deep furrows and crow's feet
it passionately sings.

My mirror speaks to me with stark
honesty, with truth, without shame
that once youth is gone and beauty fades
it's the end of the waiting game.

But do I listen to my mirror, that silly
mirror on the wall
do I listen to my mirror that has
no voice at all
do I listen to my mirror with eyes
that cannot see
or do I really look and listen
to the mirror whose reflection is me?

Like the Angel's Kiss

Like the angel's kiss
That caresses my cheek
And brings good tidings from above
Like the delicate kiss of the butterfly
It brings the message of love.

Like the strong, forceful kiss of the
Surf as it sings
Like the kiss of the gentle dove
They bring back to me the thought of
Earthly things
Of your kiss and you, my love.

Like the mother's kiss that warms the child
She brings comfort and joy to everyone
Her only thought is to bring happiness, good cheer
And to find her place in the sun.

Like the father's kiss that brings assurance
That makes the child feel secure
It is a kiss of strength, of hope
Of the essence of a love that is pure.

But alas, I am not a mother or even a
Father to be
Thus my wish is the wish that the
Kiss that we kiss will
Sow the seeds of a new life
That all the world will see.

But this dream may need a miracle, a miracle,
I pray it will be mine
One day soon, not too late, for there
Is not much left to my allotted time.

For the days drift by too fast, much too fast
For mere woman am I to see
That this hope of my dreams can bear fruit
Or be crushed
In these years that are yet to be.

Still in my heart of hearts I know
That if my dream does not come true
I must find peace within my saddened
Soul
And then, my love, help you.

And then finally, before the clock strikes twelve
I must lift up my eyes in prayer
To the stars, to the moon, to that
Special voice, I pray though I know
Not what is there.

And then I wait and wonder
Will the stars twinkle down
Will the moon shine, will
The happy message come from above
I do not know, I only know
There will always be, our deep
Abiding love.

I Wish I Were

I wish I were I wish I might
be the one chosen to carry the ball
to run and run and run and win
to give my strength, my heart, my soul, my all.

I wish I may I wish I might
be the creative one who fulfills his dream
the artist, the sculptor, the writer, no matter
what's important is to be part of the team.

I wish I may I wish I might
be the one who finds the cure
that helps lost souls to live again
to make sure their lives endure.

I wish I may I wish I might
have that wonderful gift of joy and laughter
that can change what is serious and
dull and sad
to what is light and bright, forever after.

And I also wish my life would have meaning
I wish my life would somehow be pure
I wish the way would be relieved
of all pain and clutter and tears
no matter, no difference, rich or poor.

But if all these wishes turn to naught
then at least can I be
the chosen one with good health, spirits high
and the one who walks in gracious dignity.

Do I ask too much, am I ridiculous?
Mere man, are my wishes all in vain
to think that perhaps for the second time around
I might win again?

Or is my life just too short
too brief to make roots, to plan?
And perhaps, these roots are just a futile wish
a dream, and the idle imagination of man.

Yet I will not yield, I must not yield
dare I try to make my life turn out to be
the wishes that I wished, the dreams
that I dreamed
a world of love of peace of hope
worthy of immortality.

When I Dream

When I dream do I dream
of the shadowed world
that lies in the darkness of my brain?
When I dream do I dream of that
spirit world
that creates happiness as well as pain?

Are my dreams just the dreams of my fancy?
Or are they the songs that are yet to be
sung?
Or are they the instruments of that darkness
world imprinted on the banner of my soul
waiting waiting to be chastised and hung?

Should I let my dreams be just dreams
here and now?
Should I believe only what I can touch and feel
or should I reach out to enfold that
shadowed world
and make it mine, make it mine,
make it real?
Or should I wait 'til those songs have been sung
the final songs that have yet to be?
For they may still be the greatest songs
of love, of beauty, of man and
nature's harmony.

Does Your Smile

Does your smile fit the day
is it bright as the sun
is it pure as the first shimmering snow
is it a smile of satisfaction and happiness
giving pleasure, wherever you go?

Or is it the false smile of secrets
the smile of unhappiness and pain?
Or is it the almost smile of a tortured heart
reaching out, reaching out in vain?
Or is it a window that reflects the inner soul
that will help one weather a storm
til it's blown away and replaced by one from the heart
in the early morn?

Make your smile fit the day
Let it glow like the sun
Let it flow from within to without
Let it dance in the wind
Let it sing, let it shout
Let it tell the world what it's about.

Make your smile fit the day
Throw your cares to the clouds
Let it touch the moon
The stars and reach out 'til the day is done.
Let it be your best, let it
Be your all, let your smile
Be the smile that captures
Everyone.

The Moment

The moment I was conceived, then born
My song began to sing its song
And as each hour, each day past
The music the melody continued on, and on
Indeed, the die was cast.

It sang the words of good, of bad
True or sad, of the blacks and whites
And greys
My melody refused to stop, I thought,
And would go on forever and a day.

But alas as the years flew by, my
Song was covered with dust
And as each hour passed it sang
Only what it must.

Oh where is the truth of my early song
Where is its honesty?
Why do I feel it's been covered with muck
And is no longer the true song of me.

Thus, should I tear off its cloak, shed
Its layers of greed of self
Rid the world of what I see
Before it's too late, bare the soul bare the
Heart and show what my song used to be.

Then once again I will sing my final song
Once again, I will stand tall and true
Once again, I can let my song touch
All nature and man
From early morn 'til dusk,
'Til the day is through.

And once again I can shout "Hallelujah,
Hallelujah"
My song has not been in vain
For immortality has allowed it to
Touch man's mind and heart
Over and over and over again.

Why Wait

Why wait to open up your mind, your heart
Why wait 'til the last hurrah
Why wait 'til the game is over and through
And for others to give their last ta ta!

Why wait 'til the tree is almost bare
Why wait 'til the winter's frost
Why wait 'til the earth is dry without care
And the vital things are almost lost.

Why wait 'til the petals fall from afar
Why wait 'till the grass is no longer green
Why wait 'til life loses its sparkle and essence
And like a star burns out and is never seen.

Why wait 'til the spirit can no longer soar
Like the mighty eagle soars on high
Why wait to spread your earthly wings
Like the delicate and exquisite butterfly.

Why wait 'til the last bell has sung
'Til the voice can no longer sing
'Til the spirit no longer wishes to try
And all life has lost its "zing."

Why wait, do it now, touch it now
Feel it now, love it now, why wait
To be all that you should be
Why wait, why wait, why wait
To learn the essence of life's mystery.

'Tis True

'Tis true that all I've ever had
My thoughts, my pen and my paper pad
And as I sit upon my chair
Ideas seem to fall into place out of the
Atmosphere, out of the air
But then I also sift inside myself
To fathom thoughts deeper than sinew and skin
Deeper than the moments of years gone by
I sift and sift and sift again, for I must
Endeavor to win.

'Tis true my pen must fill my pad
With creativity, concepts from everywhere
But how this process works, I do not know
For creativity is mysterious and so uniquely rare.

Thus, when the moment comes
The clock strikes twelve and my thoughts
Are ready to fulfill their fantasies and dreams
I ebb and flow with the tide of my
Soul as it becomes an integral part of
The team
And then I ride with the tide
Run with the wind, sound the
Clarion horn.
Dance with the stars, talk to the Universe
Perhaps, perhaps, a new creativity is born.

Is My Glass Half Full

Is my glass half full or half empty
I ask myself
As I survey my world from without
And within
And in the passage of time, will the
World be all mine
Filled with platinum and gold, or plastic and tin.

Will my world feel the sunshine
Touch the rain and snow, caress the clouds,
And feel the joy of spring
Will it stop to view the buds that bloom
And the wonders of nature that each new
Season brings?

And will I bless each day as I pass through
With positives, not negatives, with an urgency
For all I love
With a spirit of strength that understands
The humanness of humans and the
Message from above.

Thus, perhaps, at last, I will see my glass
Not half empty, but half full
Reflecting courage to reach out toward the sun
Touch the snow, feel the rain
Throw away the negative, take hold of the positive,
And give life a chance to renew itself
And begin to live again.

He Listens

He listens, he talks, then he listens again
to the many silences between my world and thoughts
to the how's and where's and why's and when's.

And then his years of study and know-how
help him to understand what he doesn't hear
or see
as he tries to reach my inner thoughts
and find the essence of me.

And each week at the appointed hour
I quietly find my chair
to relate the events of the week that has passed
to reassess my problems, to clear the air.

But some days all seems lost
the brightness fades away
and there I sit 'til something breaks through
then words tumble out as he listens closely
to what I have to say.

And then after months of searching and probing
probing and searching for who I am and what I want to be
the chains break loose, begin to dissolve
and at last I'm on my way to be free
to do the things I've always wanted to do
to reach out as far as my eyes
can see
to be my own man, to be my own self
to be me, to be me, to be me.

The Creative Spark

What is the creative spark
Where does it start, where does it begin
Where, oh where, does its seed come from
The mother, the father, the closest of the family
Kin.

But try I must to understand my role
The why's and wherefore's the words not mentioned
In between
The touch, the feel, the spark that helps me
Fill the pages up with
Words and sentences I have never seen.

Emotions run high, nerves become taut
A fervor grabs at the very essence
Of my mind and soul
And I am caught in a web not of my own
That reaches out far beyond the humility and subtlety
Of a human's role.

Yet, there I am, it begins and then it's over
And I am free for an hour, for a moment
For another day
Until the process starts all over again
And I, the slave of creativity, am verily
On my way.

My Chair on Wheels

Here I sit in my chair on wheels
I wonder do they care
Or do they choose to flit like the
Butterfly
Free in the windless air.

You're old they say, too old to think
To dream
They turn away in despair
They do not know I still feel young and vibrant
And ready to take on all that I might yet
Have to bare.

Oh where are their eyes, for they do not see
Where are their ears that only hear what
They have to hear
Why do they even come at all
Wouldn't it be kinder, just to stop
And not appear.

Then perhaps, I might have a chance
To reach out to another chair on wheels
To find another human who cares and thinks
And feels
To share love and respect and gratitude
And build a friendship beyond compare
With one who truly understands
The how's and why's and when's
Of his and my wheelchair.

27

Perhaps

Perhaps one day soon, my love, you will be sorry
One day soon, all too soon it will be
Too late
I hoped with all my heart, I hoped you'd understand
And help to reverse that appointed date.

I do not know what makes you turn
Against all that's tried and true
I only know that you must create your own hell
And make me prisoner as well as you.

And as the years go by, rigidity sets in
And fits you like a glove
The yes's turn to no's even before
The questions are asked, my love
Don't you see you lose, the game is over
Before it's begun
With your destructive ways and attitudes
No points can ever be won.

Then why not open your mind and heart
Why not change the no's to yes
Why not listen to your loving friend
Whose role is to know what is best.

Then perhaps, you can change the appointed date
And make your life worth living.
Change the no's to yes, try again and again
Before it's too late, too late for giving.

It Would Have Been

It would have been enough for me if you said
You loved me
It would have been enough for me if
You said you care
It would have been enough for me to hear
You say, you will, you will
And make my world human blessed, a
World indeed quite rare.

It should have been enough for you if I said
I love you
It should have been enough for you if I said
I care
It should have been enough for you to hear me
Say I do, I do
And make your world one of happiness,
A world beyond compare.

But strange, we humans, we crave too much
And our greed has no ends, knows no bounds
For it seems that should have and would have
Is never enough
As we grab for the golden ring on life's merry-go-round.

It Would Have Been Enough

It would have been enough when you
Brought me the key to that darling house
It would have been enough when you
Gave me the car
It would have been enough when you
Surprised me with my first mink coat
Then dazzled me with that diamond from afar.

It would have been enough when you asked
Me to change to that estate by the sea
It would have been enough before you
Bought the plane
It would have been enough for me to hear
You say you love me, need me
And walk hand in hand down lovers' lane.

That would have been enough, my dearest, enough,
without
All these treasures of man
For the only gift I truly wanted
Was your strong and abiding love
Each day every day from the moment you and
I began.

And It Came to Pass

And it came to pass on the night of
The first falling snow
That I looked in your eyes and fell in love
And you became my friend, not my foe.

And it came to pass on the night
Of the shimmery moon
We plighted our troth, repeated our vows
Not a month, not a week, not a day
Too soon.

But now alas, you are seventy-four and I am sixty-five
We have lived a lot of living, but are
Blessed we still survive
We have seen almost all there is to see
Almost all there is to do
But dearest friend there is still much
Left to give
In this world that constantly changes from
Black to white, from old to new.

Yet it came to pass on that night, that
Very special night when our lives
Touched four score and ten
That we repeated our vows and pledged our
Love over and over again.

For the love that was and the love
That is
And the love that shall always be
A love from above, a love that is truly love
A love that will live on to eternity.

31

I Do Not Like

I do not like to talk to the wall
At breakfast when the day has just begun
I do not like to talk to the wall
At dinner when the day is done.

If I want to talk to nothing,
I can do that all day long
If I want to talk to something,
I wait for you, then wonder what is wrong.

For there's always something else at hand
Something else that cannot wait
There's always something else to do
That makes you always late.

But one day soon, you will open your eyes
And look for me, my love
But all will be over, I will be gone
Alas, too late, too late, my love.

I Don't Give a Damn

I don't give a damn, a damn about your pride
which you use as a cover, behind which
you hide.

I don't give a damn, a damn about your
insecurities
as you try to play the role of lord and king
and push your ABC's.

I don't give a damn, not a damn anymore
how much can a heart and spirit take
so many many years of this and still
my heart and spirit ache.

And yet, I believe my love is still there
but each day it recedes deeper and deeper
within my soul
and one day soon, it may be gone, disappear
no longer able to play its role.

I don't give a damn and yet I really want
to still give a damn
and mind the errors of our ways
throw out the hurt, begin again, let
our love flower and bloom in the remaining days.

Yesterday

Yesterday when I was young
My hands were beautiful to see
My friends called my hands the golden hands
For they could create anything, anything
From A to Z.

But now that I am old and not so young
And my hands are twisted and torn
Does this mean that my soul is still
Not beautiful, my heart still not pure
My feelings still can be hurt, after all
That I have already borne.

Thus, don't notice my hands
Look at my face, look deep into my eyes
For they reach out from my inner soul
With truth, with love, without disguise.

And then take me now for what I am
(Not what I was before) and what I've
Come to be
A human that reaches out for respect
And acceptance, for love and immortality.

Sunday

Sunday, was it just yesterday that I was
Shocked beyond repair
For I learned the spouse of my
Dearest friend
Had no faith, no hope, and did not care.

And as he spoke in bitter searing tones
I looked into his eyes to see
A human with little heart or soul
Thank G-d, it wasn't me.

The light in his heart had turned to
Black cinders
His soul had crumbled to dust
And when I took a second look
Nothing but soot was left behind
Years of neglect, disinterest and rust.

Who is this man I ask myself
This stranger of my yesteryears
Who is this man I ask myself
Whose eyes can shed no tears
Who is this man who's lost his way
Perhaps never, never, to return again
Who is this man shall I, dare I, reach out and try
Though my efforts might be in vain.

When I See

When I see do I see what I really should see
When I hear do I hear what is said
When I touch do I feel a sensuous warmth
From my toes to the top of my head.

Or are my senses asleep as I walk
Through the years of my life
Do they know pleasure as well as pain
Do they know what is right, what is wrong
And what is selfish and vain
And do they know
Of violence and struggle of trust
Of courage, of love and hate.
And how to temper and rise above, irregardless
Of their fate.

For my senses should be like the limbs
Of a tree reaching out towards the sun
Seeing and thinking, hearing and feeling, touching
And embracing everyone.

Was I Born? Do I Hear?

Was I born to live but a few moments
in time
or to live out my four score and ten
was i born to be reborn somehow
somewhere, and change the world of men.

Do I live to learn the wisdom of the ages
the wisdom of strife and pain
do i live to learn
all is not lost as
I reach out for the gauntlet of courage and hope
over and over again.

Do I see the dawn of a new day
with eyes covered with childish gleam
or do i dare to tear that cover away
to reveal man's inequities as they really seem.

Do I touch so that I may feel
the exquisite sensitivity of earth and petals and skin
or do i touch so that my inner soul
is awakened by an inner light
poised for my flight to begin.

Do I feel so that I may find an inner hope
that will give me the strength and fortitude to
survive.
that will aid me in reaching my final goal
happiness, peace, contentment, sheer
gratitude to be alive.

Do I speak only to repeat words of horror
and shock, ugly tales of
violence and low self-esteem
or do i use my voice to carry tales
of the glories of man, his desires
his hopes, his fervent dreams.

Do I hear just to hear the cautious sounds
of an ambulance, the cry of a tortured soul,
the horn of a honking car
or was I given this gift to hear the
musical beat of the wind, the rain, the
snow, and the gentle cooing by a baby
from afar.

Am I poor so I can feel the pain of want
so I can plumb the depths of my despair
or would it be better if I were rich and
successful
so affluent that my sensitivities would be
beyond repair.

I ask myself these questions as the years
moments and hours drift away.
Yet, with all that I have seen and felt and
heard and done, still no answer
comes my way.

Just one thought, one single thought,
keeps gnawing at my brain
will I ever have another chance to
make the rounds again
and if not will my core, my
essence live on and somehow, somewhere, survive
if only in another's mind and heart and soul
in this world where all things come alive.

Then say I Hallelujah, Hallelujah
my life has not been in vain
for my errors and disasters will dissolve
and vanish into the Eternal Source and
hallelujah, hallelujah my true legacy
will be reborn again.

Imperfect

Imperfect are the eyes that see
Imperfect the hands that mix and mold
The clay
Imperfect is the heart that beats an
Erratic beat
And the mind that records mistakes and lessons
Learned each and every day.

Imperfect is the voice that speaks
Of the negative and the positive
Carrying thoughts better left unsaid
Imperfect is the voice that sings
Of love, of hope, of silent victories
About which no one has ever read.

Imperfect yet pliable is the human form
That twists and turns to accomplish many things
Yet forgets itself and throws away truth, respect, and faith
In its quest for wealth and the power of kings.

Imperfect yes imperfect is my soul, my heart,
And indeed the love I bear for you
But I must try to change imperfection to perfection
In all the things I see and hear and do.

But no easy task this perfection
For time, my time moves on relentlessly.
No easy task to make the impossible into possible
To reach out as far as my eyes can see
For I am only man or woman, perhaps
The challenge is too great for me
Or perhaps, at last I know I am
Human imperfect, was and is and
Will always be.

No, I Never

No, I never lie except on Monday
Except on Monday my mind seems to lie to me
No I never lie on Tuesday
Except on Tuesday my negative soul seems
To collect its fee
No I never steal except on Wednesday
Except on Wednesday, I reach out and grab
As much as I can
And then the rest of the week out of
Guilt and remorse I become the
Perfect symbol of youth and man
No I never commit adultery, especially
On Thursday, on Thursday I try to
Remain pure and free
And Friday is the day before the Sabbath
A day for thought, self analysis, faith and
Morality
And then Sunday is the family's day
No I never, at least hardly ever
For the perfect family man I strive to be
As I begin anew to rebuild never no never
For Monday is sure to follow Sunday,
Just as A will follow B.

Do I, Don't I

Do I, don't I
Should I, shouldn't I
Dare I, dare I not or
Will I, will I not.

Have I, haven't I
Must I, mustn't I
Could I, couldn't I
Would I, wouldn't I
Am I, am I not the keeper of my soul?

Who Knows, *Quien Sabé*

Who knows why the moon winks at me and
Smiles through my window pane
Who knows why the sun hides behind
My naked soul
Who knows why my heart pours out
Its song to you
Who knows, who knows, *quien sabé, quien sabé.*
Who knows why the earth shakes and shivers
And breaks apart
Who knows why the rain soothes my
Aching heart.

Who knows why my love is endless and
Limitless and true
Who knows, who knows, *quien sabé, quien sabé.*

Who knows why I walk the path of the
Weeping hemlock tree
Why I touch and so love the flowers that bloom
Why I talk to all that lives and grows on
G-d's green earth
Of love and hope and faith
Not anger and violence and doom.

Who knows why man turns to dust
Why the wind howls through the trees
Who knows why my dreams
Of fantasy and light
Become my reality.

Who knows why the clock ticks on endlessly
And time has no beginning and no end
Why the world's movers and shakers never stop
To fix, to change, to mend.

Who knows, who knows, no one knows
Yesterday, today, tomorrow what will be
For man is only finite man and can
Never know his final destiny
Who knows, who knows, *quien sabé, quien sabé*.

Prose Poetry I

I Wait

I wait and wait and wait. Every second seems like an hour, every hour seems like six. And then I wait some more. There is an air of expectancy, of excitement, an air filled with realistic fear of a negative response, a rejection! (of my work). And yet within me, there's a pulsating quiet, a rising tension becoming almost uncontrollable, almost ready to burst.

My thoughts reach out; my thoughts reach out to G-d for strength and fortitude to hold back, to wait, to believe. My gratitude reaches out, for I am grateful and humble that I am able to find the words, the thoughts, the creative instinct to place them in the proper order on the written page.

However, with all this, the waiting becomes more difficult as each day passes; for one moment I am ready to fly away on a wispy nebulous cloud; and the next moment, my spirit is ready to crash to earth and sink into oblivion, into the seedy, gritty, grainy particles of dust.

Yes, waiting is difficult—the atmosphere is so quiet as my ears reach out for the telephone to pierce the air, for the words that will give me joy and satisfaction or sadness and a sense of defeat.

I wait and wait and wait and wait—yet somehow, somewhere, in my heart and soul I believe in what I have accomplished. And though I am a mere human, I sense that perhaps my inner feelings, my intuitions, are right and that I have created something positive, something unique, something that may make our world a better world; our people kinder, more considerate, less selfish, and less egotistical.

How it happened, why it happened, when it happened, I do not know; for it tumbles out like water from a faucet, like the rain falling from the sky, like the thunder from the clouds, like the snow on a winter's day!

Somehow, an inner warmth caresses and engulfs my soul. For some reason, a gift has been bestowed upon me in the trimester of my life. For some reason, a door has been opened, and I have been given the strength, the courage, the creative ability to pass through.

How it happens, when it happens, why it happens, I do not know. I only know that I am filled with humility, gratitude and thankful prayer that I am able to leave a pertinent and permanent message that can not only be of use to those of today but can also be passed on, handed over and shared by those of tomorrow. And yet, with all this, still I wait!

My Burden, My Blessing

The agonies of pain have no beginning, have no end. My eyes well up with tears, my heart is almost ready to burst, and my spirit holds on to the last shred of courage. Unbearable, yet bearable, unmitigating yet endurable, unrelenting yet tolerable, ruthless yet sustainable, difficult yet sufferable, unforgettable yet easily forgotten when the moment passes on and the siege is over. But still I wonder about the how's and why's, the where's, the when; but the blackboard of my mind is blank, and there are no answers!

And yet though the storm has abated and my window of sun begins to surface and once again open wide, I think that perhaps all is not lost; that I can still reach out, peel off all those layers of debris and dust, and find a moment of truth; find a concept that far exceeds the pain and agony; find an idea that gives life and creativity and positive substance to that moment of living hell!

Yet, oftentimes I wonder . . . without the pain and agony, how could I know joy and jubilation; without the agony and the pain, how could I dig deep enough to reach the essence of the inner core? The inner core that reveals a momentous truth that makes it all worthwhile. A truth that tells me that somehow in the trimester of my years, I have become an instrument of a higher source. The pen that writes on the pages of life, the computer that records the negative and the positive, the happiness and the grief, the love and the violence, the indifference and the understanding, the neglect and the concern; that I have become part of the key that unlocks those doors, and the last part of the puzzle that will find the answers—perhaps through poetry or prose, fiction or non-fiction, reality or fantasy. I do not know what my role will be. I only know I can and must be the pen that fills the stark white sterile pages of my pad with truth and light and substance; that I must be the instrument that records cause and effect; that I can and must be the intermediary through which someone out there can hear the violins playing the melodies of the angels, through which someone out there can become aware of the hopes and dreams of another's drummer's beat, through which someone can not only see the bittersweet of winter and the joyous hope of spring but also feel and understand and correct the rights and wrongs of humankind.

If I can do this, if I can reach out to accept the gauntlet, if I can be the courier that delivers the message, the key that will unlock the doors, the seedling that blossoms forth and covers the world with fragrance and beauty, then I believe my agony and pain have not been in vain, the reason and purpose of my being has been revealed and at long last I am free.

Friendship

What is friendship? I ask myself as I inadvertently reach out for my Bible of words, my authority of authorities, my mighty Thesaurus whose ability to be correct, unbiased, impersonal, and precise has never failed me in my quest for knowledge and understanding.

Quickly I turn to paragraph #927 and read as follows: friendship is a state of companionship, camaraderie with a special affinity for warmth, closeness, inseparableness, and harmony. Friendship may also be a state of simpatico, fraternity, intimacy, and staunch positive commitment.

There is more, indeed much more, but I stop so that I may repeat the unwritten words, listen and digest them before I attempt to deal with the gnawing question of whether or not this state of being can come to fruition in all or just a part of its ramifications.

At this moment, I have no answer. I am perplexed as I nod my head in dissatisfaction, for my inner thoughts are in turmoil and the dictionary of my heart and mind have opened yet another vista, has defined another panorama.

Which is correct, I wonder, the words of the prophet Thesaurus or the vibration of my mind dancing to another tune. Truly, I am confused, but in my humility, let me dissect the term friendship. Let me probe its inner depths.

Is it affection? Is it loyalty? Is it consideration? Is it love? Is it accessibility? Or is it habitual? Is it sincere, simple, and straightforward in its approach or is it complicated, secretive, and devious?

Is it all of these things, or is it none of these things? But even more importantly, does it have elasticity, a flexibility that will enable it to expand, to touch the epitome of human emotion irregardless of race, color, creed.

Is it red, blue, yellow, green, orange, purple, or a mixture of all these hues? And does it matter that it is affected by and controlled by each individual's use of freedom of choice. For when that precise moment arrives will that relationship take precedence above all other priorities, or will the second slot on the list be reserved in the name of friendship long before the encounter begins.

What is friendship? I ask again. Is it based on mutual interests or mutual needs necessary and vital to that given moment in time?

Is it selfless? Is it competitive? Is it all embracing? Or does it burst forth on specific occasions with its erratic behavior?

And is it a vital component necessary in a marriage, in a love affair, in a relationship between parents and children, between neighbors, or between those close humans we come in contact with during the working ours of our days and the years of our lives.

What is friendship? I ponder, perhaps for the last time—before I cut away at the edges, remove the outer layers of pride, pomposity, jealousy, and guarded secrecy to find the essential core.

I stop, just once more to deliberate—yes, it appears friendship does exist as a human experience—that it can reach out and touch the mind, the heart, the soul in the representation of the finest and best that one man can offer another.

Yes, friendship does exist; but then I hesitate—Dare I ask one final question?

When I am young and tender and full of hope, will this friendship ebb and flow like the tide, sometimes thrashing against the rocky crevices of the cliffs above, sometimes motionless and severe; never unaccountable, always vibrant, dependable, and rewarding.

Or when I am old and almost forgotten, will that constancy turn to disinterest? Will that reliability become neglect? Will that loyalty turn to self interest? Will that love turn to anger and irritation? Will that guarded secrecy turn to withdrawal? And will that core, that essence of friendship, this time, for the last time, crash against the cliffs, vanish and dissolve into nothingness, as it becomes one with the endless sea.

The Trees

One early evening in the twilight of my later years, I had an urge, a decided urge to take the car, drive to the botanical gardens in Brooklyn, and walk in their magical exquisite Japanese garden.

It was not yet dusk when I arrived and the sunset was about to share its glory with this tiny oasis of beauty, of creativity.

The garden was completely free of visitors, and a special calming atmosphere prevailed.

I walked for several moments and then stopped suddenly to stare at, admire, and enjoy one spectacular cut leaf maple, and next to it, a tall gracious weeping hemlock. The combination of the exquisite golden delicate cobweb leaves of the maple and the majesty and graciousness of the hemlock's cascading boughs seemed to grip my thoughts in a moment when time seemed to stand still.

I just stared at the beauty and wondrous beauty of nature, not realizing that my mind was beginning to spin its own ingenious web of fantasy.

The sun had set and the moment was perfection as I watched in awe and credulity, the unfolding of a miraculous scenario.

For the cut leaf maple was no longer a tree but had assumed the role and stance of a geisha whose boughs and branches, tender leaves had fused into a silk kimono. Embroidered in golds and silver, copper and bronze, the folds of her gown flowed like golden honey as she effortlessly adopted the role of Lady Miyoa Miyomtzu, a royal descendent of the Emperor Meiji.

Indeed, I was bewitched as the moment engulfed my senses, but as my vision moved toward the weeping majestic hemlock, I was once again overcome in disbelief, for the evergreen had assumed the stance of the infamous lady Suzu Isheygawa. Dressed in a flowing silk kimono she was adorned in blues and greens, silver and gold, the darks and lights that dramatically befit the Emperor Meiji's staunchest adversary.

I watched in awe still fascinated as I became aware of the fact that the geishas began to move toward each other and bow—and then slowly move to the beat of music they alone could hear.

But then the beat became stronger, the tinkly musical theme grew louder as their steps and movements began to form a pattern of dance completely unknown to me.

I listened, I watched as the moments enfolded into a experience almost beyond human comprehension.

But then the music stopped, the dancers reverted back to their original positions; a stillness pervaded the atmosphere, and it was over.

I shook my head in disbelief. Had this pageant really occurred? Was this just a figment of my colorful imagination? Had I become too deeply involved in my own thoughts? Or had I fallen into a meditative spell?

Somehow, I could not find the answer or perhaps, only human, I should not know the answer.

Perhaps it was a dream, perhaps it was an unfulfilled wish, my way to reach out to the wonders of nature. Or perhaps, it was only my humanness to try to touch, to feel, to become one with the universe.

Humanality

Pray tell, what is a human? What was a human? And what is the extent of the breath and scope of future human capability?

Synthesized and reduced to the basic essentials of water, blood, bone, sinew, and flesh. Given thought and imagination, creativity and sensitivity, will and desire, is the human still a composite of his special and specific originality, and do his differences outweigh his similarities?

No doubt time will prove the latter to be true, or even more importantly, untrue, for there is massive evidence that the human quality of sameness not only exists today but will continue *ad infinitum.*

If this is valid, does it then follow through that the human can and will continue to acclimate to any environment, that he can and will continue to become an integral part of its foundation in order to develop sociological, cultural, physiological tools to be utilized in his final supreme effort to find and achieve the freedom to dissolve into oblivion and become one with Eternity.

Poetry II

The Silence

The silence, that golden silence
that warms me through and through
that gives me space to mend my ways
clear my mind, pace my steps
review and understand what I can and cannot do.

The silence, that quiet moment
that hides me from friend or foe
that protects me while I sift through layers
of dust
to find the inner truth
of what I should and should not know.

The silence, that magical silence
that is mine and only mine
for without it, I cannot function
I cannot clarify the upset world
I cannot think, I cannot unwind.

Thus, each day I must set aside a moment
for that silence—to see what is right
and what is true
to sift out and weigh the differences
between the old and the new
to find a strength, a spirit to challenge
and show the world the secret that keeps me alive
and the power of silence, my golden silence
without which I could never survive.

If I Walk in Your Shoes

If I walk in your shoes, will you walk in mine
will you go wherever they go
and will you also take my thoughts and dreams
to challenge whatever I know.

If I wear your clothes, will you wear mine
with delight and appreciation of my style
and then will you borrow my "joie de vivre"
to make it all worthwhile.

Or will you gripe and still complain
about your difficulties, how much easier
it is for me
even after you've chosen to wear
my clothes and shoes
to make you into what you think you
would like to be.

But, don't you know you cannot
steal another heart, another mind
or change what is mine to yours
or cover your soul with my clothes and shoes
hoping beyond hope your choice
will unlock the door.

No, no, I cannot walk in your shoes,
no, no, you cannot walk in mine,
it can never be, it will not work,
now or ever, until the end of time.

I Don't Care

I don't care that my beauty has lost its glow
I don't care that my back is bowed and bent
I don't care that my hands can no longer knit or sew
And that other hands have to be lent.

I don't care that my ears cannot hear every single word
I don't care that my eyes need glasses to see
I don't care that I walk even slower than slow
And to get there I must push, push on unrelentlessly.

I don't care that I no longer have that total look
That my sense of fashion has lost its way
I don't care that coordination is beyond my realm and
control
Including my use of make-up every single day.

For it seems that all these things are part of youth
That fades and falls apart as the years go by
And all this, I must accept
Without the if's and wherefore's and why's.

For indeed what's more important
That the mind be sharp and clear
That it ticks like the clock on the mantle
Ticking away in my ear.

And what's more important is the spirit
That fights on and on to survive
That never gives up the battle
To stay vibrant and alive.

And indeed what's even more important
Is the soul and the message that it brings
That the game goes on, must be played to the end
'Til the clarion calls, 'til the clarion calls
Out its final ring.

Am I?

Am I half man or half woman
Are you half woman or half man
And have we always been that way
Ever since the world began?

Am I a composite of my family's genes
Are you the synthesis of yours
And are we born to follow whatever we choose
The right, the left, the in between
Or that which hides beyond the door?

Are we all half man or half woman
Are we all half woman, half man
What road do we follow and where is it written
What we can't do or what we can?

Then who is to judge, who is to
Have the final say?
For there is no right, no wrong
And there is no judgment who shall
Get the short end of the stick,
The middle, or the long.

Thus should we rise above society
To understand the humanness of man
To realize that perhaps we cannot
And were not meant to change
What is, what was, what will always be
Since the world began.

The Apple

The apple is half bitter
The apple is half sweet
And how and why and where
I bite
Can be a woeful taste experience (disaster)
Or a delightful treat.

The choice is mine to pick, to choose
The apple that is shiny and perfect and true
But do I really know what's beyond (under) the skin
What's old and ripe, what's firm and new.

So I take my chances with eyes open or closed
For somewhere I must begin
Like life, the apple can be half bitter, half sweet
And I can lose or win.

Thus, I should choose my apples wisely
I must touch and feel and see
Use my knowledge, my know-how with caution
Then wait to see what will be.

And if in the final choice, they are both
Bitter and sweet
Then know this is just one
Simple example from the world
Of nature and man
For the apple is just a symbol
Of the good and the bad,
The sweet and the sad,
And what cannot be, what can.

Why, Oh Why?

Why, oh why, was I born to feel
such frustration and pain
beyond the limits of humankind?

And why, oh why, was I born to touch
the stars, the moon, the sun
and make the whole world mine?

Why, oh why, am I the one
to know and sense the essence of the soul
to reach out to feel what is right,
what is true?

And why, oh why, do I see the
difference of humans more than others
in what they say and do?

Why, oh why, am I the one who must
bear the brunt, carry the load
with a dignity and charisma that
defies the norm?

And why, oh why, I ask, is there any valid answer
is it coincidence or a mistake of
this mad, mad world
why I was given this task
when I was born?

Yet if this be true
should I be the showcase
the balance for all the world to see
and should I carry the banner
on which is scarred the essence of my heart and soul
the banner that represents only me?

If Only

If only I were young again
with wisdom and foresight to see
what should have been said and done
so many years ago
to make me the being I was meant to be.

If only the strands of my hair were
still red, not grey
my appearance might add to my charm
and life might be a greater adventure
a more distinctive challenge in which
I could be happier, less frustrated, and more calm.

If only I could run or just walk at a faster pace
my accomplishments would add up to so much more
and I might even win the race and do
better than before.

If only I could wipe my tearful eyes and
still see the minute details of life's beauty and joy
then perhaps I might fathom the answers
to its many puzzles
without time wasted playing with childish minds,
human games and toys.

If only I could sing like I sang once before
notes high and low, with passion and flame
then my stay here might have
more meaning and beauty and contentment
and this life could be a better game.

If only, if only, there was no change
and all things could remain as they were before
then I could rock and rock and rock
in my rocking chair
without thought to ask for more.

But what's the use of If Only
for the universe will never stop
it must continue on the wheels of time
and no matter, no matter my foolish
conjecture and fanciful thoughts
for they are part of my If Only
and can never, will never be mine.

The World Is Free

The world is free
Is it, is it?

The earth and nature are free
Are they, are they?

The trees and plants and flowers are free
Are they or are they not?

The animal world, all creatures that
Walk this earth are free
Are they, are they?

The air, the sky, the sea
All are free
Are they and will they always be?

And what of all humankind
Is he free?
Is he, is he?

Or is he just one infinitesimal unit in the hierarchy
Of the universe, or is he the appointed catalyst
Of the Great Unknown
That is all-giving, all-seeing, all-feeling,
All-loving, all-purposeful, all-powerful
And all-knowing, far beyond man's capacity
To know and understand
Far beyond human comprehension and mortality.

Too Old Am I

Too old am I to make the choice
Whatever the problem may be
For indecision, confusion has gripped my heart,
Crossed my path, convulsed my mind
For all the world to see.

Too old am I to think young thoughts
That are covered by the rusty cobwebs of
Despair,
For I have lost the challenge, the struggle
Of anxiety and hope,
And my soul seems beyond repair.

Too old am I, am I too old to erase
The past, listen to the silence of the present
And begin all over again—
Gather wisdom, hope, and courage, change
Imbalance to balance and finally, finally
Become a man among men.

Tears

Are my tears the symbols of sadness
Or are they the darkest expressions of
My salty soul.
Or are they the release of my inner spark
That nurtures my strength to go on and on and on
Until I reach my ultimate goal.

Are my tears the symbols of happiness
Or the simplistic emotions of conflict, regret,
And sorrow.
Or are they tools that will free my
Heart, my mind, to overcome all the days of
My tomorrows.

Are my tears the jewels of anticipation and
Hope
The diamonds of courage that will never let
Me fail.
Or are they the watery moonbeams that
Cleanse and remove the layers of dust
And grime
But alas, to no avail!

Yet, somehow I believe these tears of humankind
Must be the catharses, the secret, the key
That will unlock the door to freedom,
To faith, to strength, to life, to fulfill
My ultimate destiny.

Let Me Tell You

Let me tell you how much I love you
Let me count the ways
Then let me speak of those special moments
Of each and every day
For our love will become everlasting
As the days and years fly by
And we will survive the onslaught
Of youthful anxiety, foolish concern
And the tears that make us cry.

And then before the final chapter has been
Recorded
Peace of mind and ageless wisdom
Will answer the how's, the wherefore's, the why's
And our love will achieve immortality
We will never, never have to say good-bye!

Now

Now that I am seventy-three
What do I have to prove anymore
And where should I go, what should I do
To open up the eyes of the world, to make
The cannons roar?

Now that I am seventy-three
Have I reached a point of no return
Is there nothing left to challenge
Are there any lessons to be learned?

And now that I have reached the age of seventy-three
Will I make it to seventy-four
And if I do should I live in darkness
Or open the windows wide,
Before someone, something
Slams that final door?

Happiness

Happiness is like a fleeting cloud
that drifts effortlessly through the sky
nuances of color, waves of light
and darkened shadows
that reflect the positives, the negatives
of the how's and where's and why's.

Happiness is like a silken thread
that's woven throughout the fabric of life
strong as the eagle, sensitive as the
perfumed jasmine
it counteracts pandemonium, conflict, and strife.

Happiness is but a teardrop of thought,
a delicate theme, a soft murmur of the soul
a melody, a symphony that will guide me
to fulfill my goal.

Happiness is yet a rainbow
that emanates from on high
bright, illuminating, effervescent
it may last for only a moment
then it fades away and dies.

And yet, in totality, happiness is perhaps,
just a dream.
a fantasy, a short-lived truth that can never come to be.
for its essence too quickly dissolves
into the melting pot of humankind
where it loses life and human identity.

My Love

My love is endless like the eternal sea
As it flows through each moment, each
Hour of each year
My love grows in depth, in strength,
In wisdom
Yet, like the sea, it will never disappear.

My love is like the red, red rose
Whose essence pervades my heart, my mind, my soul
And like the beauty of the rose will never fade
As it endeavor to fulfill its glorious role.

My love is like a silken thread
Woven into the fabric of my sinew, my skin
Strong, resilient, it will never self destruct,
It will never shred
If the game is lost or if I should go on and on
And win.

For my love has no beginning, no ending
Its human reality may last but for
A moment in time
Yet, alas without Alpha and Omega
It cannot be, will never be mine,
Eternally mine.

The Palette of the Universe

The palette of the Universe is mine and mine
alone to see
the wonders of all nature
and the things that are yet to be.

The patterns of the Universe resemble the
roads, life's roads on which I twist
and turn
tell me, will truth prevail if all else should fail
will I ever or never, never learn?

The cycle of the Universe
is it infinite or is it beyond
the human limitations
of man
and are there any answers, can we
emotionalize, intellectualize, rationalize
just how it all began?

For man is but a thread of silk,
a grain of sand, the whispering wind on
a summer's day
knowing yet unknowing
profound yet apprehensive
rational yet pragmatic
will he ever know the answers to the puzzle of
the Universe
will he ever find the way?

"The Words Of"

"Be silent and know, therefore, 'That I AM'
observe Nature, the Universe, and realize
that I exist.
Plunge deep into the essence of your heart,
your mind, your soul, and discover that
my precepts are based on truth, love,
wisdom and understanding.

Think positive thoughts, not negative vibrations
and remember I am your Mentor, your
Protector, your Liberator, your All.

Live each hour, each minute, as if it were
perhaps, your last.
Then live each day of each year with feeling,
patience, humility, compassion—to prove
you are an urgent example of the fact that
your humanness has not been in vain—
that My laws, My teachings, My precepts have
become an integral life force of your very being,
your humility.

For then—when that propitious moment
appears and you must cross over to the other
side, I will bring you peace, not anxiety,
contentment, not retribution, succor, not
anguish, euphoria, not torment—for I
am the Alpha and the Omega and—
I will be with you today, tomorrow,
and forever more!"

Shall I?

Shall I listen to the voice that poignant voice
that sings within my aching soul
shall I listen to the silent words of my
constant feeling heart?
Shall I try to rekindle my strength, my
faith, my courage, before I lose control or
find the essence of an inner force to conquer,
to win, to fulfill my appointed part?

Shall I follow the stars, the moon, the
sun on high
shall I gather that light to brighten
my limited human world
and shall it be my guide, my shield,
my banner that will come forth with
majesty, it will graciously unfurl?

Then, shall I take the seeds of my birth,
the flowers of my youth, the unfulfilled
dreams of my golden years
endeavor to sift, sift, again, and again
'til I find the way without humiliation, without
regret, without fear.

For too soon, the should-have's, the would-have's,
have disappeared; time has melted away
and all my efforts have dissipated
into the melting pot of humankind
while my soul waits patiently,
impatiently for that recorded day.

My Eyes

My eyes have seen the wonders, the glorious
wonders that I cannot understand
and my eyes have also seen the blacks and
grays, the in-betweens of sadness, of a
world beyond the damned.

My ears have heard the cries of nature,
the cry of humans, the unfinished song
of those who have lost their way
of those who cannot find the answers to the
winds of darkness, of havoc, and decay.

My voice has spoken words and
sounds misused in a hurricane
of truth.
Devoid of wisdom, positive reflection, unselfish
contemplation—I, the piper, must acknowledge
the ultimate cost—
a living entity, inhuman, vicious, and uncouth.

And yet, I often wonder are these tools
these precious gifts, mere happenstance, the
ironic trust of fate
or are they ours only ours—a simplistic means
to learn, to improve, to create?

One world, one cosmos where all
humanity is free
to speak words of gold, hear
the sounds of angels, see the intrinsic
beauty of man and nature, just a
reflection of you and me.

How Blind

How blind am I that I cannot see
the ignoble trials and tribulations
of a world that is mine?
How insensible are my passions, my
feelings that I am unaware, cannot
comprehend or recognize the degeneration
of its vital signs?
How obtuse am I that my mental acumen
cannot think, cannot heal the dilemma
of the human plight?
And why can't I or another find the answer,
the means to mend what is wrong
and finally, make it right?
But, perhaps, there are no viable solutions,
possibilities or impossibilities to the puzzle of
humankind, the riddle of you and me.
For man is but a mortal, a grain of sand,
a fleck of dust, a split second in
the dynamic sphere of Universal immortality.

If I

If I cannot be what you want me to be
Will I be chastised and thrown away
And if I refuse to be what you would
Like to see
Will you discard me and leave me to decay?

And alas, if I'm afraid to be what
You would hope for me
Will you defiantly slam the door, throw
Away the key
Or will you in wisdom self-analysis
Finally, admit you would like to change places
That in essence, you would really like to
Be me?

How?

How shall I live the rest of my days, my love
How shall I find the way
When shall, I give the last hurrah,
And admit, confused and lost, it's almost
The end of my day?

How shall I spend the moments, those
Fleeting moments
When we can no longer think, or dream, or care
When the hours and days melt into nothingness
A quiet void, a quiet silence that is
So hard to bear?

How shall I know my cup is half full,
Not half empty
And will last only 'til the human darkness
Comes
When I feel no more, my senses can no
Longer soar
The game is over, my Karma, my destiny,
Has won!

Won what? I ask in humble innocence
Is there more, something more beyond what I
Feel, I know I cannot see.
And does finity become infinity
Where you and I, my love, will meet again
Where you and I will forever be?

I'm Not Mad

I'm not mad but is the world mad?
The world I can and cannot see
I'm not ashamed but is the world ashamed
of its violence, greed and lust, its damnation, its
vicious atrocities.

I'm not confused but is the world confused
as it idly surveys the human condition, man's
madness goes astray
then wonders who and what will stop this
roller coaster of insanity that grows in power,
in momentum, hour by hour, day by day?

I'm not at fault or am I and all the others
at fault
who see only what they choose to see
who ignore greed, self-indulgence
devil-may-care attitudes and refuse to face reality?

That we of the human race are one
have a mission on this God's green earth
to cleanse our minds, our hearts, our souls,
to utilize the total measure of each
and every man's worth.

Then perhaps, the tides will be stemmed
the irreversible will be reversed, the storm
of inhumanity will be repulsed, rebuffed,
will finally cease.
Madness will be replaced by sobriety
confusion by positive objectivity
greed, self-indulgence by sharing and caring
and at last, at long last, the world,
our world of humankind will move forward
to find happiness, contentment, and everlasting peace.

Here I Am—I

Here I am without a heart, without a brain,
even perhaps, without a soul!
Here I am lost in time and space
without conviction, realism, truth, and courage.
Can I, will I be able to fulfill my creative role?

Here I am alone and bewildered as I reach out
for the sunshine, the light,
that will sustain, guide me on my way.
Teach me how to correct the ills of humanity,
however, wherever, whenever come what may.

Here I am with mortal flaws, latent scars that live
in the very essence of my soul.
Errors of the flesh, greed and desire.
Can I change the impossible to possible
and find a true measure of control?

For the days are numbered, the hours short,
time seems to be drifting away.
Is it too late, too late to regain a mortal heart,
a mortal brain,
an immortal soul before the appointed day?

My Soul—I

My soul is like a withered bough
That moves cautiously to the sounds of the whispering
wind.
Knotted and gnarled with strength of purpose
It survives, it rises above all nature
Beyond all human things.

My soul is like a sword of steel
Strong as the arrow, pliable, yet gentle, as the first bloom
of Spring.
It will go forth to challenge the cruelty, the viciousness of
humankind, the
Abnormal, the neurotic, all the woes that life can bring!

My soul reflects the ebb and tide
The celestial music of the ocean's roar,
Gentle and serene, without mercy
As it rushes toward the murky shore.

My soul is like the eternal clouds
That fill my eyes with beauty beyond repair
But like the clouds, it reaches out to those who are lost,
To those who no longer care
To touch their lives with a message of courage and hope
To right all the human wrongs
To change the negatives to positive
To create a world in which all true souls like you and I
Can live, can endure, can belong.

My Life—I

My life is in "Your hands, Oh Lord"
To mold to form like the sculptor molds his clay
To teach me humility, wisdom and the courage
To live life to its fullest
Every second, every moment, every hour of every day.

My destiny is in "Your hands, Oh Lord"
To guide me, nurture me to forever light the way,
with patience, strength,
Endurance, rise above
And conquer, hate, violence, blasphemy and decay.

My soul is in your hands, Oh Mighty One
The yesterdays, the todays, the tomorrows
That may or may not come to be
For born of dust, I must return to dust
How or when, only human, I do not know, I cannot know
Written in the sands of time, it is my destiny.

Let Me

Let me stretch my heart across the sky
To keep you safe, secure, and warm
Let me spread my love like the butterfly
To cover, to protect you
From the very moment you were born.

Let me give you strength of mind and body
To enhance and support your elusive evasive soul.
For the road is long and treacherous
The choices plus and minus
As you strive to reach your ultimate goal.

And then let me give you the key
to share all that is within me.
Not for the present, not for tomorrow,
but forever, and a day.
Then I will have no regrets, perhaps,
Your life will be more meaningful, my love, as
Destiny guides you on your way.

Prose Poetry II

Prayer

My destiny is in your hands, Oh Lord! Thus teach me, acknowledge me, guide me through the hours of my days and days of my years.

And though I am but a human, let my eyes see goodness and beauty. Let my ears hear the music of angels, words of wisdom, compassion, let my heart know love for mankind, nature, the universe and let my soul, my spirit soar high above the clouds with strength, courage, and gracious humility.

Teach me to love, not hate, find joy not pain, contentment not adversity, silent peace not anxiety and endless dissatisfaction.

Lead me in the path of truth and righteousness. Then, enable me to understand there is no ugliness, but only what man creates out of cruelty, greed, selfishness and ignorance.

"Oh, Omniscient One," teach me to be kind, to realize my cup is always half-full not half-empty. And if I am moving too fast, slow me down, but if, like the tortoise, I am procrastinating, show me how to improve my earthly lot. Then let me succeed, feel the positiveness of earthly living so that I may appreciate the differences, realize the fruits of my labor.

"Oh, Mighty One," guide me, nurture me, give me time and space to err. Knowing I am only human, imperfect, do not chastise me but allow me to recognize my mistakes, learn and move forward with the wisdom and knowledge to achieve, to succeed.

For then, and only then, my steps would not have been wasted, my human life would not have been in vain. For in my heart of hearts, in the very essence of my soul, I know I am and will always be in "Your hands, Oh, Lord" to mold, to sculpt, to guide, to renew.

"So, it is inscribed on the Tablet of Destiny that only You are all knowing, that only You can decipher for man is mortal, his days on Earth are counted. Born of dust, he must return to dust as his soul becomes one with the river that has no beginning, no ending as it passionately flows on and on and on into Eternity."

Blinded

Blinded by the senseless truths of man,
I see yet I cannot see.
Blinded by the amoral platitudes of man, I search and
reach out but cannot find my chosen identity.

Blinded by a cosmos of a thousand faces
hidden in the abyss
of a defenseless weary mind
that questions where shall one go,
what can one do to change the unchangeable,
find the means to correct the mistakes
and leave the negatives behind.

Blinded by the complexities of a world lost in the vortex of
a mad magnetic storm,
I ask, I meditate, are there any options?
Can the human race
find the key, the strength, the wisdom,
the faith to survive the onslaught,
to once again be reborn?

Or will man forever be blinded
like those cultures, lost souls who live no more
whose wasted minds and hearts
dissolved into nothingness, into grains of sand,
leaving a legacy, a world,
no better than it was before!

Friendship

Can you mend a friendship
As old as the chestnut tree
Can you gather all the chestnuts, hurts and recriminations
Put them all together, find a new approach, a fresh
identity?

Can you forget the pain, the anguish
the sadness as deep and wide as the ocean's
roar? Can they be covered with mental cobwebs,
stored away and labeled . . . forgive,
forget, go on as you were before?

Can you bury all the negatives,
unearth the positives and endeavor to begin anew,
search and look for another human
that can be unselfish, considerate, forthright
and true?

And then, at long last, this new friendship,
can it live on and on in my memory of
time? Can it replace the one I've lost,
can it be one of satisfaction and happiness,
can it be mine, can it be mine, can it be mine?!

What's the Difference?

What's the difference between abled and disabled?
It's the difference between yes and no
And it's a realistic look at that long
Treacherous road ahead
Whenever and wherever I choose to go.

What's the difference between independency
And dependency?
For no longer is the cane my friend, my guide
For I have lost the precious gift of
Freedom
As I patiently, impatiently, wait for someone
To help me, to constantly be at my side.

What's the difference between abled and
Disabled?
It's the difference between faith, courage,
joie de vivre and hope
Of keeping the positive not the negative
Winning not losing as my soul reaches
Out for inner strength to rise above and cope.

What's the difference, it's the difference
That makes all the difference, for the
Struggle never ends.

Friends begin to ignore you
Strangers see you as abnormal
And believe you can never mend.

Yes, the difference is traumatic
For, only you and I know what was lost,
Light and sunshine replaced by darkness
And shadows
A world, yours and mine, never the same
Again, regardless of the cost.

Yes, that difference there is no other
That touches the heart, the mind, the soul
That tears away at the essence of life
Leaving emptiness and despair as its goal.

And even though perhaps, you and I
May triumph and perhaps, our dreams and
Hopes may come to be,
There will never be a replacement
That transcends the difference—that
Difference that represents you and me.

Where, Oh Where?

Where oh where is the land of Nashirigawa
that land of Eternal Spring
where existence has no beginning, no ending
the cosmic song never ceases, the bell
never tolls, never rings?

Where oh where is that island of never, never
where birth and death, time and space are
but an illusion of man
a silent thread woven into the fabric of the
Universe
strong yet illusive, vibrant yet untouchable
sensitive yet impenetrable, vital yet consistent
no ending no beginning, on and on and on
from that precise moment when it all began?

Where oh where is that haven of enlightened majesty
where negativism disappears into oblivion,
into nothingness, the plagues of humanity cease
where pain and torment, anxiety and hopelessness
are replaced by quiet sanctity, man can
take his place in the hierarchy of the Universe
where there is fulfillment, contentment, and peace?

Yet, only mortal, I dream, I ask, I wonder,
is there a land of Nashirigawa
where sunbeams and moonbeams tenderly
touch my mind, creep into my silent heart,
my naked soul
where all my yesterdays, todays, and tomorrows
are one; for there is no ending, no beginning,
only a clarification, a resolution of man's
appointed role.

The So-So Club

Well, here I am. I've just turned seventy and somehow automatically without provocation, yours truly has just joined the "So-So Club!"

How are you? So-So. How do you feel. So-So. What's new? Well, things are slightly chaotic . . . the world is falling apart, but mind you, everything is okay. Well . . . when I really think about it, it's just So-So.

So-So, So-So, but after the last So-So, where do you go from there? Tempus fugits and life is changing rapidly.

The hair has turned to white. The wrinkles have taken on new horizons, and the perfect body has lost its resiliency and is thinner than thin, fatter than fat.

The walk is slow, slow, slow. The back is no longer right angles with everything else. And the eyes, the eyes though still bright and clear sometimes appear slightly blurry, watery, and confused.

Years 1923, 1993, time has taken its toll. Little things have become big things and the still littler things have almost immersed the mind into abstract nothingness.

Daily life has become an obstacle course, and each step is

more challenging than the next. The bills mount up. The rejection slips have no conscience, and the phone rings constantly. And how much longer can I adhere to and repeat that senseless inane So-So reply.

Where does it begin and where does it end? I ask myself. But then I note if the So-So's stop, I am no longer in existence, I am nothing. And I will become a non-entity . . . thus, born of dust, I will return to dust with just a long history of So-So's in between.

Small So-So's, large So-So's, good So-So's, bad So-So's, clever So-So's, innocuous So-So's. Happy So-So's, Sad So-So's, positive So-So's, negative So-So's, and then add all the So-So's that disappear into oblivion! Thousands of So-So's . . . in fact, I do believe I have been chosen Chairman of the Board of the elite So-So Club. And come hell or high water, I have no other choice, no other option, for it's 1993 . . . who else can walk in my shoes? Thus I must accept the inevitable, gather all of my years of So-So wear and tear, of experience, expertise, knowledge and wisdom in order to succeed. And then if the challenge has been met perhaps, some day, one day if good fortune smiles, someone up there will remember and appoint me President of the International So-So Club!

Oh, to Be

Oh to be whole again, whole again, whole again,
is this a dream that can never come to be
to walk free and equal to the beat of
the Universal drum?
Is this a sinful wish, a selfish whim,
perhaps, an impossible reality?

Oh to be whole again, once again,
with my head held high as I did long years before,
not an outcast, not a stranger, this is my
wish if I had one wish, could I,
would I ask for anything more?

Oh to be whole again, whole again, whole again,
to have youth and strength and passion
to play the human game
to find the essence of one's heart and
mind and soul to rise above and give
credence to my humble name.

But alas, it's sad, perhaps, my wishful fantasy
to be whole again, it will never come to be
thus accept I must the inevitable, then go on
and on and on to understand, appreciate, and
love the intrinsic values of my unique identity.

Who Am I?

A tree, a leaf, a star, am I
A bud, a cloud, a drop of rain, am I
All these, yet nothing, for who am I,
    and am I what I am not!

A gushing stream, a silent lake, an ocean's roar, am I
A clap of thunder, a bolt of lightning,
A blustery storm am I . . . all these things, yet nothing.
For who am I, and am I what I am not!

A blast of winter, a pelting snow, the first crocus of spring,
    I am.
The golden blossoms at dawn, the perfumed orchids at
    dusk,
But am I and am I what I am not?
For I am all these things and more.
Yet, I am nothing; I am all these things, yet, I am
    something . . .
In the magnificent glorification of Nature,
In the catastrophic devastation of the Universe,
In the never-ending,
All-encompassing,
Continuous cycle of life and death
That is eternal, who am I?

Clouds II

Elongated appendages of fluid cobwebs intricate yet simplistic, indescribable and inexplicable, appearing then disappearing into nothingness, they move, they change continuously to a rhythm only the Universe knows, a rhythm that has no beginning, no ending.

Lights and darks, ovals and rounds, triangles and oblongs, misty granulated puffs, they are similar yet dissimilar.

Balanced, yet unbalanced, structured yet unstructured, they change unknowingly with complete abandon. Free and unencumbered, they seem to flow out of each other and into each other, always conforming to a Universal Code that is and is not, that is not and is.

A miracle of lights and shadows melting into one dimension or several. Ever so slowly and almost invisible unless one watches with a cautious eye, an alert mind, an aesthetic soul!

Pinks and lavenders, whites, blacks, blues, greys . . . mystical, indescribably beautiful, unanswerable, a spectacular moment suspended within a moment of time.

Always different, always the same; always the same, always different.

Soft and feathery, dark and dense and menacing, fragile and tender and compelling. How fortunate that this panorama of nature in all its glory is mine to behold!

And though only a human, I cannot fully comprehend many Universal concepts, I am able to watch the clouds in a summer sky, feel the wonder of Nature, appreciate the innate essence of the Universe as I fantasize, hope, dream, and believe in the Glory of Nature and the personification of Man!

Does Man

Does man live in a prison of shadows,
A fool's Paradise, an illusion of his youth?
Is man limited, can he overcome the darkness,
Pierce the mask of humankind
To find the unadulterated truth?

Does man live in a world of time and space
Is he only as old or as young as he thinks and feels?
And does he have the power,
The momentum to change the darkness to light,
Find the proper balance and replace his youthful fantasies
With concepts that are wise, mature and real?

For it is self-evident,
That the threads of human existence can
Never be broken, they are an integral part
Of the Universal song,
The symphony that has no beginning, no ending.
Man, Nature, the Universe,
On and on and on into Eternity!
They will be sustained and forever remain
Where they belong.

Aren't You Glad It's Friday?

Aren't you glad it's Friday,
will wonders never cease,
for the days of Saturday and Sunday
will erase all trauma and tension
and bring joy, renewal, and inner peace.

Aren't you glad it's Friday,
a semi-colon to anxiety and concern,
a time to change disorder into order, use
creativity to gain wisdom and knowledge, find the
means to continue to learn.

Aren't you glad it's Friday,
a brief respite from the daily problems of
anguish and despair,
a time to find freedom to search for the
answers and find the means to survive,
to conquer, to repair
the ravages of humanity that need time
and space to mend
the havoc, the confusion, the uncertainty,
the entropic message it sends.

Thus thank goodness, it's finally Friday,
perhaps, a moment for miracles, man's conscious
effort to reverse the irreversible, take charge and
reach out for the golden ring,
then find the energy to reverse Nature,
the Universe, to listen to the Voice of
Eternity as it sings and sings and sings.

Can I See?

Can I see through the mask of humanity,
Or is it just an illusion of space and time
Is birth and death, a beginning,
An ending
And can the world, my world ever be
Mine, all mine?

Is there proof of reality, am I living, can I
Prove and know I'm real
And is my Universe the same as yours
Do I see, and hear and speak as you do
Can I know what you and you alone can feel?

For though we are the same, we are separate
Connected yet unconnected, different we dance
To the same cosmic song
That has no beginning, no ending—thus I meditate,
I wonder, can humanity like Nature continue to be reborn.

Down by the Poolside—I

Down by the poolside, that's all I ever hear,
gossip, gossip, gossip, loud and shrill and clear,
who broke a leg, a hip, who had a fall,
whose husband left her, was it Levinson or
Levine, somehow, I can't recall.

Who visited the specialist, neurologist, podiatrist,
dermatologist, was it kidney, liver, or gall,
X-rays, CAT scans, bone scans, tests, tests, tests,
those hospitals, those medical gurus surely had a ball.

Who had a facelift, the laser, that pill, what's its name
that melts away the years,
but it hasn't been approved by the FDA
is it worth the risk, six weeks in Europe, and
can it obliterate anxiety and fear?

And then, after a lengthy pause, bridge, jewels,
designer clothes, travel—pray tell, what other
subjects could there be—
down by the poolside, gossip, gossip, gossip,
thank goodness, I'm relieved, I'm darn glad
they're not discussing me!

What Do You Do?

What do you do when the world no longer
Has significant meaning
What do you do when life seems to fall
Apart at your feet
From where do you gather strength, wisdom, knowledge,
Courage to mend all fences
And perhaps for the last time, go forth, reach out,
And endeavor to win, to compete?

What should you do when the romance, the challenge
Of each day has filtered into nothingness
When the sunbeams and the moonbeams can
No longer touch the heart, the mind, the soul
When day is night and night is day
And you think you feel, you know, you
Realize you've lost all measure, some measure of control?

What do you do when there is no
Longer a purpose
A reason, a desire to play the
Human game
Should you give up, throw in the towel
Sit and sit and sit, let
Your world self destruct into oblivion
Just sit and sit and sit 'til
Destiny calls your name?

Do You Know?

Do you know what happiness is?
Have you forgotten how to smile?
Where is your sense of humor, your essence,
Your joie de vivre
Are they covered by cobwebs, layers of dust,
Bitterness and hate hidden away deep
In your spiritual and mental file?

Do you know what peace of mind, contentment,
Well-being are?
Do you really know how to live?
Or are you just existing, waiting,
For the blackness of night to cover your wasted
Days and hours and years
While you hide and purposely forget not to forgive?

Do you know when your glass is half full,
Not half empty?
When the pluses outweigh the minuses
As you live and survive,
The tribulations, the disappointments that touch
You, affect you each and every day.

But do you also know that with strength,
With courage, you can find that glimpse of sunshine,
That rainbow of happiness, if you only want it, need it,
It's there within your reach, it's really
Not so far away.

My Garden (Opus XXV)

Here, I stand in my garden of fear
On my island of no tomorrows
Here, I wonder and wait and wonder
What the winds of time and change will bring
Vengeance and hate, lust and greed,
Pain and suffering, days and years of sorrow.

Here I stand in my garden of love
On my island of many tomorrows
For I believe in the goodness of man,
The truth and honesty of our world
No need to beg, to steal, to lie, to cheat, to borrow.

Here I stand once again in my sacred garden
On my island of safety that is no more,
For the moment has come to break the ties
Assume the burden, find the courage and strength
To become wiser than before.

For, for the last time,
I must be alone in my garden of fear
And try to walk in the footsteps of man,
With the full knowledge that you are still there
As you always were
From the moment our world, our garden, began.

A Legacy of Love

It must have been pre-ordained, or perhaps, in my world of believing, deep within my soul, in my subconscious, I was aware of one simplistic fact: that when you are born, it is written!

And so it was, and therefore, it began. I was twenty-five years old, unmarried, "an old maid," they said, "there's no hope," until one of my father's clients suggested a weekend at Grossinger's Hotel.

Thus, there I was on the Saturday of Memorial Day weekend, sitting on a bench after lunch. Waiting, for what? We were talking, my parents and I, wasting time, making polite conversation, until a stranger stopped to say hello, smiled, and introduced himself. His name was Harold. Pleasant, fairly intelligent, and affable. Little did I know that at that specific moment, the clock had stopped, a new chapter was beginning to unfold. When, where, how, I did not know—but my parents knew—how intuitive; for they fell in love with this attractive stranger at first sight. It was mutual, for he later confessed, he also knew. Not only that but in the months that followed, he became a son to them, even more than their very own.

Yes, we met, we talked for approximately ten minutes and I did not see him again until Sunday afternoon, for I didn't meet him at the casino the night before as I had promised.

Clearly, he was disappointed but did not give up when

he requested my phone number, my address, and could he visit me when I returned to my home in Weehawken, New Jersey. Why not?

Funny this stranger knew, but slightly naive and innocent, I didn't. In fact, when he got home, he informed his mother he had found the one girl in the whole world he wanted to marry. As a result, an accountant—an Internal Revenue Agent—he quickly developed a plan of action.

He called Thursday morning, visited Thursday evening on and on and on and on and on until he proposed on August 19th. On and on and on and on until the day of December 25 when we were married.

Of course, a typical male human, he became nervous and scared when he revealed "everything is going too fast" and I answered, "I'm not making you come!" I guess I was sassy and independent! But loving every minute of it!

On and on and on until December 25, 1947 arrived. I chose the day because I felt all the world was at peace. Yes, all the world cooperated but not the weather. It snowed twelve inches, the wedding almost didn't happen, almost! A success, it was the beginning, the onset of the most wonderful adventure, most glorious experience of my life!

A seven-week honeymoon, we were happy, ecstatic, Atlantic City, Quebec, bound for somewhere, anywhere, it didn't matter, we were in love! He even more than I; intuitive, he seemed to understand me, even more than I did. Intuitively, he realized in my subconscious development, I needed space and time to search within myself to enrich my heart, my mind, my soul. For I was still innocent, a seed that had to grow; a bud that had to bloom, not yet, but soon, for my creative spark had to be ignited and given the chance to envelop my entire being, to bring light to the world.

But alas, it was 1947 and a woman's place was in the home, cooking, shopping, having a family, a college degree, post graduate, a potential lawyer, interesting but clearly, incidental. At least that's what my beloved thought. Little did he realize my thoughts. The plan of action I was giving birth to beside the arrival of my wonderful daughter, Robyn, who eventually became Dr. Robyn. Yet with all that I still had a necessity to reach out into the world, an inner drive to create, to bring forth something else beside my role of wife and mother, to fulfill whatever had been written that moment I was born!

Indeed, I was in a hurry, but had the patience to wait for my dear husband to realize I needed his positive approval even more than life itself. Finally at long last, it happened, the windows opened wide and the sun began to shine.

Over and over, I proved that my knowledge, my feelings, my vibrations, gave me a very unique talent! Whatever I saw, whatever I touched, I knew the level of difference. Again and again it worked. For example, one afternoon, we were riding on Third Avenue when I yelled "Stop, there's something in the window," and as a result, I purchased eighty objects of Japanese Art that I really didn't need. But the next two hours would prove to my darling husband and friend, that "I already knew my onions!" When we returned home and unwrapped them, a decorator called and made an appointment, which resulted in the sale of all but one, and an increase in a much larger sum than we anticipated. We hugged, we kissed—I had won the war when he realized finally what was necessary for my survival!

And so, I began to buy and buy and buy, nothing stopped me even when at the fairly young age of forty I had my first attack of arthritis. In bed for seven weeks, the doctors said I would never walk again. Dragged from one office to another, from one hospital to another, to find the only solution was to untangle my emotions, to find inner strength and the hope that it was vital to live, not exist, that I had to go on, and on, and on.

The Coliseum Antique Show, The Madison Square Garden Antique Show, I tried everything! And I loved every minute of it—Tao Yin Gallery—we shared each experience with joy, especially the moment when Harold gave one of my most beautiful Japanese art objects to a stranger who cried out, "I love it, but can't afford it!"

It was a gift from his heart and an expression of his love. In fact, his love reached out even more when as a result of a fall, I spent four months in Helen Hayes Rehabilitation Center. Every day he came in the rain, in the snow, in the cold, cold winter, come what may, every day to hug me, kiss me, wipe my tears away when rehabilitation became so difficult and painful! But unbelievably another door began to open, Harold had found the key, my difficulties were no longer a burden but a blessing. I began to write again!

And even though they told me for the second time, I would never walk again, and even when they brought the wheelchair into the kitchen, I would not accept the finality of their words.

As soon as they left, I said take that damn wheelchair out of my kitchen, I will never use it! And then I added, I am going to walk, I am going to write, I am going to lecture, I am going to survive and do everything! I will not feel sorry, it will be a blessing, not a burden, I will be positive, not negative, my glass is almost half full, not almost half empty.

Fort Lee High School, adult education, Fairleigh Dickinson University, Bloomingdales Newark Museum, Etta Ress Institute in West Palm Beach, I couldn't stop. It was a challenge and I loved it. Harold was so proud when I lectured. He attended classes asked questions, but this was just the beginning. I began to write up a storm: "The Enigma of Satsumaware," "Zinkye," "An Anthology of Poetry,"

116

"Feelings," "The Legend of Nashirigawa," "Yabu Massa," and then a series of lectures, "Why Poetry," "The Fasunation of Oriental Art," and "The Difference Between Living and Existing," and to my chagrin two students walked out, they couldn't face the truth.

But Harold was always there to smile, to laugh, to guide me, tell amusing stories, to comfort me, to give me support even if I decided to fly to the moon, and when he held my hand for the millionth time, I knew as always that he would never forsake me, that he would walk with me every step of the way for fifty-four years; or until that split second when he would have to cross over to the other side. Even then, I knew in my heart, I would never, never be alone.

We had shared everything, the good, the bad, the happy, the sad. We had lived a lifetime together, and I was blessed. This man of humility, of elegance, of grace had been my friend, my benefactor, my lover, my everything.

This man who always put me first on his list, who always told me how beautiful I was even when I developed wrinkles and was bent and bowed; who always boasted about my artistic endeavors, my creativity, my uniqueness. This all-giving, beloved man who was my champion, my Samurai warrior, who honored me, protected me, guarded me from suffering, embarrassment, and pain.

Indeed he was and will always be my "Guiding Light," my "Guardian Angel." Truly I am blessed! Could I have asked for anything more????? Could I have wished for anything more????? Could I have prayed for anything more?????

Tic Toc, Tic Toc, Tic Toc

What is time? Tic toc, tic toc, tic toc! Yesterday, we were one; we spoke, we touched, we looked into each other's eyes.

Our days, our moments were filled with love, companionship, sharing, and caring. We laughed, we cried, we communicated. Words were unimportant, just being together was the perfect "Prescription" for happiness and complete fulfillment.

But time never stops, time moves on unrelentlessly—tic toc, tic toc, tic toc. Today is gone!

It is the dawn of a new day, and the pain and agony of tomorrow has not only descended upon me, but has convulsed my soul, dissolved it into nothingness. For in the split second of time, you are gone, my love. You have crossed over to the other side! Tic toc, tic toc. Today a reality, tomorrow a memory that slowly pulls at my heartstrings, tugs at my soul, transforms me into perhaps, someone I do not know, I cannot recognize. Perhaps, a stranger, a lost soul that has become a human robot. Unrecognizable, paranoid, antisocial, filled with deep roots of traumatic hurt and denial—searching for a quick fix that doesn't exist.

Moments, days, months, years of pain, agony, hopelessness, and despair, without mercy. Tic toc, tic toc, tic toc.

And yet throughout this catastrophic upheaval, there are those who endeavor to give counsel: "Have patience, time will heal, time will be the catharsis that will enable you to endure, to rise above, to find peace, be positive, and go forward!"

And then, there are those who tell you to discard the rituals that have somehow become vital to your very existence, to your sanity—for yesterday, a world of love—tic toc, tic toc, tic toc—today, a world of nothingness!

Over and over and over I hear the tic toc, as I reach out for spiritual, mental, religious sustenance. Over and over and over I ask: Can I let go? Can I go on? Can I rise above not what I was, but what I have become?

Can I return to yesterday? Can I change today? Or can I make yesterday tomorrow? Are there any answers? Are there any solutions?

For what is time? It tugs away at my heartstrings. My spirit fades; my tears turn into a river of stones.

Loneliness engulfs my soul, my emotions. Nothing is left except a void that cannot be filled!

I reach out, but no one is there; except perhaps, when I pray, when I engage in a fantasy of my own creativity. A fantasy that allows me to talk to my beloved even though in my heart, he has crossed over to the other side.

Yet somehow, there is comfort in the knowledge that I am not alone; that I have not been deserted; that my love will always be there to cover me with a blanket of sunlight, will always be there to protect me from the dark clouds of the unknown, from the distant world that I, a human, cannot fully comprehend.

And yet, somehow, there is comfort in the realization that my beloved's smile has given me the courage, the empathy, to go on, to face the world, that his eyes have looked into my soul and have given me the inspiration to find an outlet for my creativity, that his silent words have aided me in the belief that my thoughts are special, my intentions are pure, my G'd-given talent is worthy of recognition, and that the essence of my being, my inner strength, will give me the urgency to conquer fears, renew my faith, reach for the ultimate goal of acceptance and personal satisfaction.

And so, tic toc, tic toc, tic toc, life continues on, and I must find the meaning, find the way to live, not exist, to once again become human—to love, not hate, give not take, to reach out—to once again, open my eyes, my heart, my mind, my soul so that I fulfill my beloved's hopes and dreams and can be what he wanted me to become, so that my life, the remainder of my days, may be touched by the golden rays of the sun, touched by the silvery shadows of the moon, pierced by the penetrating brilliance of the stars. For time has no beginning, no ending—yesterday, today, tomorrow, tic toc, tic toc, tic toc, tic toc, on and on and on and on into eternity!!!